Trauma:

Becoming A Healed You

Moonsoulchild

Trauma: Becoming A Healed You

I hope when you read this collection you leave with another perspective... because that is what my intention always is, to share my perspective through my experiences and my healing journey. I'm not here to tell anyone how to heal. I know hearing triggering things that hit close to you may open wounds that still cut deep... but that is the first step in my healing process... confronting the uncomfortable, so please, read this as if you're in my head. Don't read it as a direct hit toward you, because I don't know you or your journey... I can only speak on my own. Fill in the blanks as you read, and help heal what you need to... only you can do that.

Be your **savior**.
Be your own *redemption*.

Trauma is the memory we all wish to forget... that somehow we can be healed and freed from the dangerous thoughts that forever haunt us. Trauma is our story in the most hurtful way because so much pain is attached. Trauma has broken us and shaped us. Trauma has haunted us throughout our lives and they end up repeating through connections if we don't heal. There's no running from your trauma, it will always find you and highlight everything you tried to bury. There's no cure for those traumatic experiences, they will forever live within you but the key is to heal the part of you that holds so much weight and no longer allow those demons to take control of you. Set boundaries. Unlearn patterns. Confront your triggers. The layers of healing are painful and deep, it can be brutal and overwhelmingly unpleasant to face everything you've worked so hard to hide. You will always be disappointed if you think healing means forgetting your trauma. Healing is facing it without fear to set yourself free of the weight it holds over you... and will continue to in everyone you come to know.

A letter to my trauma:

I said my goodbyes to the things I couldn't keep holding onto, I was tired of letting you tear me apart. I was exhausted trying to find ways to fill voids through souls knowing I could never build homes within broken walls and improper foundations. I was searching for someone to heal me but the bandage never stuck. I wasn't aware I had to be my own redemption. I felt hollow, echoed by sadness, and hidden in spaces I couldn't seek comfort in. I created a bond with trauma, I became codependent on getting my heart broken. I became reckless with my heart when I held it hostage from growth. I thought since someone broke me they deserved to compensate me for my loss. It was a messy game I played to be loved. I thrived in sadness, it was the only feeling that wasn't fleeting.

Write a letter to your trauma:

_____

_____

_____

_____

_____

_____

_____

_____

_____

_____

_____

_____

_____

_____

_____

_____

_____

_____

5 Positive things about my Trauma:

1. *Trauma* taught me I'm stronger than it's made me believe, that the barriers built to break me only made me stronger. It was all in my head, the fear of never forgetting made me suffer more when I decided to hide instead of confronting. I conquered the fear and became fearless.

2. *Trauma* gave me a vision I never had before, the viewpoint of many layers of myself — the broken, the lost, the searching, and the fearless. I went through many layers to discover the beautiful soul that I buried deep... to finally embrace, nurture, and love every part of my being.

3. *Trauma* helped me realize I couldn't save anyone from their pain, I couldn't heal them from their hurting. I needed to love them and allow them to find themselves on their time but if it's meant for our

paths to be broken... I had to accept the truth about not being destined for each other forever and understand our time together was our story.

4. *Trauma* helped me see every side of the story, not just the pain I endured but the pain that surrounded every story involved... to know every feeling is valid and I'm allowed to feel how I do without regrets.

5. *Trauma* gave me a different perspective on how I look at life and connections. It helped me forgive myself for putting up with a lot I didn't need to... but understand no one is obligated to my forgiveness if they hurt me in any form. I don't need to forgive them because that forgiveness won't take the weight of the trauma I hold. The goal was to let the weight of the trauma go, I did that without forgiving.

5 Positive things about your Trauma:

1. _____
   _____
   _____
   _____

2. _____
   _____
   _____
   _____

3. _____
   _____
   _____
   _____

4. _____
   _____
   _____
   _____

5. _____
   _____
   _____
   _____

When it came to *my healing journey*, I learned one thing… I need to be positive. I couldn't be a victim of my trauma forever if I wanted to be free of it. I couldn't use my trauma as an excuse for my deceitful behavior… I couldn't hurt people because I was hurt. I couldn't put the work on others, to heal me, that burden was too heavy to carry. I couldn't project my anger onto everyone. I couldn't project every time I felt triggered. I couldn't allow broken pieces from my past to find a place in the place I wanted to make light. I couldn't keep trying to heal in an environment I was asking to be healed from. I needed to do the work. I needed to make the decision. I needed to be uncomfortable in every aspect… to grow… to bloom into the soul I present today. I needed to be this soul worth choosing to be. I needed to believe it. I needed to love myself. I dragged myself through the darkness to breathe. I knew I'd forever live with the haunting of my trauma, which I could do… but I refused to allow it to kill me slowly. I had to make a compromise.

When it came to my healing journey,
I learned one thing...

_____

_____

_____

_____

_____

_____

_____

_____

_____

_____

_____

_____

_____

_____

_____

_____

_____

Before my healing...

I was constantly triggered. I reacted off impulse. I always needed the last word. I was extremely insecure... which projected throughout every connection. I thought someone could heal me, or even distract me from feeling unworthy and lifeless. I wanted so desperately to be loved I settled for those who couldn't love me. I played the victim when they hurt me. I knew they couldn't give me what I wanted but I thought maybe they could learn to... I held onto any hope I was given. I wanted everything good for the wrong reasons. I hurt people who were good to me. I ghosted people I loved because I couldn't communicate anymore. I was living in this dark place I made myself comfortable in... the only place I called home. I was filled with rage. I was riddled with anxiety. I was lost and I couldn't define myself... I couldn't find myself. I allowed fear, anger, and resentment make a monster out of me. My trauma conquered me.

Before my healing...

_____

_____

_____

_____

_____

_____

_____

_____

_____

_____

_____

_____

_____

_____

_____

_____

_____

_____

_____

1 A.M. Feels

I don't have the tools to heal you but that doesn't mean I don't sympathize with your experiences. This healing journey of mine has been intense, honest, and uncomfortable. The pain is sometimes unbearable but I bandage the wound and make the time to hold myself together. I make the time to hold myself accountable the same way I seek forgiveness. I know there are two sides to every story-- sometimes I'm the victim... sometimes I'm the sinner. I had to stop blaming my past for the constant revisit of trauma that continued the cycle of how I bonded with everyone. Chaos lived in the shadows of my heart and it thrived every time I thought I had the sources to heal someone when I couldn't fathom facing my mirror of deception and agony. I thought healing someone would make me worthy. I thought if I could give someone what I didn't have… what I couldn't give myself, I would somehow find a sense of purpose. I was preaching but wasn't practicing. I feared my reflection. I believed the stories when it came to who I was to everyone. I tried creating my own narrivate but failed. The lost era was the time most dragged out… the times I dreaded. Sometimes I wish someone could have healed me. Sometimes I wish I had these words to save me.

<u>Writing is therapy</u>
Self — love is therapy
Self-- care is therapy
Music is therapy
Laugher is therapy
Bliss is therapy
<u>Nature</u> is therapy
ART is therapy
Crying is therapy

What is your "therapy"?

_____

_____

_____

_____

_____

_____

_____

_____

_____

_____

_____

_____

_____

_____

_____

_____

_____

No Superpowers

I attracted broken souls so much
I thought it was my calling
to save, fix, and heal them.
I thought if I could
they would love me.
I caught myself
drowning in their trauma
I ended up almost broken
trying to mend them together.

Your unresolved trauma
will end up hurting everyone
Including you
In the crossfire,
when you try and love them
with a broken heart.

I couldn't go to war.
I couldn't fight someone's demons for them.
I couldn't take their pain away.
I couldn't heal them from their trauma.
I couldn't provide what they yearned for.
I couldn't be the void.

I can have empathy.
I can love them.
I can listen to them.
I can be there.
I can be their peace.

I needed to be present more than trying to save them. I couldn't stand anyone I loved being hurt but I needed to learn my boundaries—and it wasn't healthy to try to heal someone and leave them with the impression I could but only fail them. I couldn't promise someone anything I couldn't deliver. It wasn't healthy for me to believe I could but always let myself down. I needed to redirect the focus of love…more toward the person and not the idea.

You either *heal your trauma*
or forever let it **haunt** you.

The message that bloomed

Stop projecting your trauma onto everyone
when you don't know what they've been
through. Don't assume you're the only one
battling something. Don't play victim to
every situation you're triggered by. Not
everything is a direct hit toward you. We're
all healing. I'm over the "victim" behavior
your whole life. A lot of us are battling
demons and trying to unlearn patterns,
cycles, and behaviors. Have empathy. It's
wrong to attack someone because you're
triggered by something you created a
narrative about. Stop projecting!! If you
decide to soak forever in your trauma and
never allow yourself to heal, you will
always play victim to your trauma. let go of
that mindset.

Healing is terrifying... yes, but it's the best
option. It may hurt to unpack all the
memories and those dark things you keep
hidden but project onto everyone who
doesn't deserve it. healing means facing

everything and accepting it happened. You may never have a reason. To have a healthy relationship with yourself you need to heal. to have any kind of relationship with anyone you need to heal. do whatever work you need. Therapy. Journaling. Self-love. Whatever makes you feel comfortable to unpack. Do the work. It's important.

I don't walk around triggered by everything. I don't project my trauma onto everyone. I don't create narratives to make people feel bad for me. I am the only one who can do the work. I am my redemption and savior. I'm healing every day. My demons aren't anyone's responsibility. A lot of the time people take my writing pieces and create a narrative (because they're triggered) and blame me for being wrong and hurtful… when they twist my words projecting their own trauma. it happens often… It's not my responsibility to heal you. Being a victim of your trauma doesn't give you the right to bully everyone. It doesn't give you a right to tell me I'm wrong or I'm "entitled" because I don't understand everyone's trauma… I'm not meant to. I only have room for my own. Get out of the mindset everyone needs to heal you. get out of the mindset that you won't ever be healed because you don't understand what happened to you. you may never understand or know why. But healing and moving on no matter how painful it will be, or it will always haunt and control you.

I wouldn't have been able to write this if it didn't come from a close place. I needed these words too—the days I wasn't too kind. The days I assumed when I shouldn't have judged. The days I could have held more compassion. The days I feed into every trigger. The days I projected my pain unbearably and ruined every good thing that came my way. I needed a little tough self-love to cure me. I need honest conversations with myself. I needed to unpack. I couldn't keep ghosting my trauma—suppressing it only made it stronger.

Healing is a never-ending process that may scare some people. Some believe that healing is the ultimate goal and that when you're healed you'll be a new version of yourself and forget every piece of you that was broken. Healing is letting go of the weight you're carrying but leaving it somewhere in your heart that you'll forever hold so you won't repeat or accept that form again. Remembering our trauma isn't a sign of being unhealed because you'll never forget. Allowing your trauma to control you and fearing how beautiful the unknown could be will destroy you.

The healing process starts after you let go and move on from everything you're trying to heal from. You can't heal from something you're not ready to walk away from and be honest with yourself about why you should.

Don't let love keep you around trauma. Don't let love hold you back from your growth. *Don't settle for love.* You will love many souls in your life, it's not healthy to hold everyone to the standard forever. Some will go.

Healing starts from within you. The trauma you've faced. The burdens you're carrying. The regret that's holding you close. You need to let go of everything that makes you feel like you're not enough.

Work on your trauma.
Work on your karma.
Open up and face it.
You won't heal if you hide
…it will only eat you alive.
Heal your soul
feed it with
what it needs to grow.

-   *let yourself bloom*

Past emotions I still hold close:

The times I was trying to identify with who I was and who I was trying to be. When I didn't feel comfortable in my skin because the time someone recognized me, it was for my acne or weight. I developed a bad habit of being critical of my appearance and looking for acceptance. I wanted to fit in and nothing I had made me feel complete. I didn't wish to stand out because my timid soul was afraid of the outcome. I thought fitting in would make me invisible. I thought being shy and reserved would make me unknown. I let the opinions and voices of others let me dictate my vision of myself. I live with the constant issues battling my love for myself when it comes to my appearance. I've come to a place of loving myself and embracing that love but still find myself falling into the same feeling

when I get a breakout or start to bloat.
That's the only time I wish I was perfect.
Being too skinny made me too visible.
Having acne made me less attractive. Being
shy made others believe I was mute. I was
afraid of the world because I didn't know
how to love myself. I still struggle with
having a voice because those times always
revisit when I feel threatened.

Today,

I know it's a feeling that will pass so I don't
let myself stay too long in the moment. I
realized distractions are healthy. Just
because it frequently visited me didn't
mean it controlled me any longer. I won
when I turned dwelling into a reflection…
so I can access the story without letting the
pain and fear attain me… to no longer allow
them to suffocate me.

I was once lost--I hurt good people because of my unhealed past trauma. I had pure intentions that went tainted when I felt insecure or felt I wasn't good enough.
It was all in my head. I had to find peace in my solitude without attaching loneliness.
I had to heal on my own.
No one could do that for me.

I retracted my promise to healing
when I denied my trauma.
Comparing the weight
of my demons
only robbed me
of *peace*.

A LETTER TO MY FIRST HEARTBREAK

I didn't even think it would be possible to fall at 15, but with you it was easy. You were a dear friend to me; we talked on the phone every night. There were miles between us, but we made it work. It was bliss until it wasn't. I remember dealing with so much, not knowing the meaning of love but somehow I ended up loving you. I think this is where it all began, my chase for someone to love me too. You were my first heartbreak. We were young--there was so much we didn't understand. Being someone who closed myself off to the world, I opened myself to you; we seemed to get each other. I didn't know my battle with anxiety then, as I learned how you feared your mental health. Two young adults searching for love and knowledge. Although you struggled with your mental illness and I struggled with my identity, it brought us closer.

Loving you was complicated; one day you loved me and the next you didn't. I thought I was helping you through your battle; as I'm trying to save you, I didn't realize it was impossible; it wasn't something I could conquer. I didn't know it was my first toxic encounter, and I let those unhealthy patterns exist for years to come in every connection made after. I don't blame you for your mental health; I tried to stand by you, I tried saving you. I don't blame you for the hurtful things you'd say or the times you couldn't recall; I tried to comprehend. I went to bed with many tears. I wondered many times why I couldn't make it work. I blamed myself for a lot that became of us because of my need to rescue; I believe it started with you. My heart broke knowing there wasn't anything I could do to heal you. My heart broke knowing there wasn't anything I could do to make this work. I didn't realize it wasn't meant for us. We were two lost souls that related and confused it with love. I don't hold our fallout as a burden; I just hope you're doing well out there in the world. I just hope you finally saved yourself.

A LETTER TO AN OLD FLAME

I convinced myself I loved you through
those years of wasted moments trying to
make you mine. I was young and naïve, and
you used that to play me, to get me where
you wanted me. I let you ghost me and
come back when you pleased because I was
love drunk off the idea of what we could be.
I let you live a double life because I was too
blind to see clearly. The words you spoke
had so much meaning until you never
followed through. I waited, I prayed, and I
had faith it could be us. I blamed myself for
a lot of the times it didn't work out when it
was your time to take the blame. I never
understood why you'd waste your time if
you didn't love me or if you didn't care. So,
I kept trying to analyze a love that wasn't
loved at all. More so, a love of convenience.
You kept me around to make yourself feel
good and then left me to wonder what
could become. It was wrong the way you
played my heart, but it never missed a beat.

Two-sided story

I always chose to stay. So, shame on me.
Shame on me for letting you walk all over
me. Shame on me for letting you get into
the depths of my soul that no one has ever
touched. Shame on me for putting up with
your mind games. Shame on me for
believing love would ever live within you.

Shame on you for always misleading me.
Shame on you for always making me feel
we had a chance. Shame on you for keeping
me in your fantasy of what we could be;
when you had every opportunity to set me
free, you chose to let me dream.

MY FIRST TIME

I still remember saying no,
while you kept going.
I was uncomfortable
but you didn't care,
It's like you couldn't hear me.
I was in pain physically;
my mind had no recollection
of the moments,
I couldn't process a thought
I only felt the pain of you inside me.
I couldn't tell you
If it crushed my soul,
I didn't realize you took advantage
of me emotionally.
At that moment,
I was confused
I was love drunk off the idea you planted; so I
never thought you raped me.
The love I had for you
blinded me.
I thought your love was going to save me
Instead,
you intoxicated me
killing me slowly,
you were no hero,
I was fooled.
You were the devil, disguised.

Coming out

I don't think there was a time
I stopped time to announce
I loved the same gender
In an intimate way
If you knew, you knew
I didn't keep it a secret
nor did I scream it from the rooftops
I loved who I loved,
the ones who couldn't accept it
tried to justify it
tell me "it's probably a phase"
The ones who love me,
It never changed their perception of me
why would it?
It shouldn't need to be a secret
but we live in a world
coming out is the fear
we're made to believe
Love doesn't conquer
when it comes to the same gender
you're made to believe
you're a disgrace
you're in a phase

you don't deserve the same blessings
because your "**love is love**"
Isn't love at all,
so we hide,
and throw away the key
to the deepest secret
we're forced to keep
because being free and open
could mean a death sentence
The words overplayed still hurt
their unresolved trauma and hate
within their heart, they can't undo
So they must choose you
to break down,
to mold
to make you into someone you're not.
So I said,
fuck "coming out"
I don't owe anyone an explanation
when it comes to love

To continue this pattern of loving people
who were good at faking
who were great at leaving
To continue this pattern of trauma
pattern of behavior
when I ghosted people
because I couldn't handle for them to hurt
until I hurt them more
by not letting them feel worthy enough
to understand
I wasn't worthy enough to be good to them
to love them
the way they deserved
because I was a coward
because I couldn't love myself enough

Those are the words
I always wished to hear from you,
instead,
"I don't know" was your reasoning

I blamed myself for
all the failed relationships
chasing people
who were only be good at leaving me.

It cost me years of suppressed trauma
broken situationships
and my own toxic traits.
But if I had to choose,
I would choose not knowing over
hearing you say, "I don't know"
It's like you were confirming
I was worthless.

Sonder

I can't take back how I felt all these years
because my feelings are valid. You ghosting and
coming back without a reason left a bruise on
my heart, one that won't ever fade. I wondered
for years whether I wasn't enough or who it was
that ran you away. I need to live without getting
answers to my questions, and I'm at peace with
living without that piece of me. Parts of you
were a mystery, you were good at stayin' low.
That emptiness in me turned to anger, one that
was brewing in me for so long. I didn't once
consider you could be projecting because of
your demons. I know it's more complex than
just the truth being told. You would need to dig
deep and unleash those dark memories you
wished to forget. You would need to release
emotions you shut off from, some so, were the
reason you left. You would need to face
everything again, after reliving it and also
running from it your whole life. I tried to think
of every scenario because I thought it would
hurt less, but the truth left me emptier. I guess
we'll always be bonded by trauma- you eluding
your demons, and me, paying for them.

Trauma Bonded

I was searching for someone to save me, I put the burden on you, and everyone who passed through my heart. Our brokenness connected us; we were both searching to feel something.

I feel we suppress a different kind of trauma when it comes to settling for the bare minimum of someone because we want them to love us. We make excuse after excuse because we feel like this time will be different. A dozen second chances only to lose them all, to lose ourselves in the end after all. Nothing good comes from opening old wounds, just room for them to cut deeper.

The healing process is never over. Our trauma will always live within us. The more we grow the more we heal. We aren't our trauma... it doesn't define us, it's to teach us we can conquer anything.

WE DEVELOP TOXIC TRAITS

Through our life experiences. We develop toxic traits when we choose to hurt someone to level the same pain they made us feel. We develop toxic traits when we overlook the pain someone inflicts on us and use "love" as an excuse to stay. When love is never enough or is it an excuse to be treated less? We develop toxic traits when we get lost in someone else, forgetting our worth along the way. We develop toxic traits when we project our pain onto everyone who comes into our life because "we're broken" from past trauma, and it's not their job to fix or heal us. We develop toxic traits when we decide not to unlearn our old patterns, behavior, and traits we once knew. We all have been toxic in one way or another; it's not something to be proud of, but it's something, to be honest about. Unlearning them is crucial; it brings you to a new level of clarity and peace. No longer hurting yourself or anyone that walks in your life. You'll know what kind of energy you are around and what not to accept. It's a beautiful thing when you free yourself of those demons.

Healing is scary when you're faced with all
your pain and trauma upfront. We always
wish to suppress our trauma, it seems easier
than facing it, easier than reliving it.
Healing isn't meant to be easy,
it's meant to leave scars
to remind you how far you've come.

Unspoken Truths

One thing we always get wrong is refusing to face our trauma and taking account of everything we've endured before we quickly try and reach the finish line with someone else. I don't think we often talk about the stigma surrounding falling for someone else so quickly after walking away from someone we spent a lot of our lives with, but we often don't talk about how sometimes we left emotionally way before we physically were capable, and there's nothing wrong with that… especially after all the pain we let impact our way of thinking, loving, and growing. When we're in a relationship in the beginning things usually feel like a miracle, we feel as if we finally found a gem we've searched so long for, but once that relationship reaches its time you grow apart and things become unbearable, but you refuse to walk away because times get hard, you were taught to fight for love. What isn't often talked about is that we're never fighting for love, we're fighting for something that's no longer love, something no longer connected to us. *No*

one talks about how it's okay to let go, **it's okay to move on**. *It's okay to know that the love you once felt can't be revived and it's okay to leave it as you once remembered it.* No one talks about how it's okay to start over with someone new, even soon after, or if it was calculated when you were emotionally distant from that once-upon-a-time love. There's no rule book to falling and loving… when you find comfort in someone there's no wrong way to do anything.
Never jump into anything when you don't know your intentions, or because you feel lonely, or haven't recovered from the heartache of anything holding pain over you. It is rarely talked about and when it is, it seems cliché, but no one can promise you the world, it's not something that can be given. Putting that much trust in someone will only disappoint you if they leave, as they take the whole world with them you feel worthless. When that **magical** love comes around, they won't need to promise anything, **they will feel like home** and that will be enough.

Breaking free from your trauma is the beginning of another journey. Healing is messy, it's not immediate peace. It's time to unlearn everything you've adapted while holding onto the trauma for so long.

Developing a bond with desire from the trauma of never feeling good enough. Nothing brings the soul more loss than the need to be found. The need to be felt. The need to be heard. Holding onto people after they let you go will only burden you. Heal the broken parts of you before you search to fill a void only you were meant to fulfill.

Letting yourself escape the pain and trauma will keep you in that dark place subconsciously, you won't see it but you will repeat these behaviors to everyone who comes in after. There's no such thing as a distraction for healing, you suppress and become a toxic risk to your mental health and everyone who loves you. It's not about finding love with someone opposite of what you've loved before… it's about healing the version of you that holds the trauma and pain that attracts the wrong ones. There's a difference between being trauma bonded with someone and having a bond with trauma. It's important to look deep inside because it all starts with you. If you forever run from the demons that haunt you, you will forever accept the love that only hurts you.

Blame game

I thought the trauma
that surrounded my heart
was me
surviving my karma.

Your spell had me lovesick

Set a short-term goal:

Letters to self

You found temporary pit stops to souls who needed saving and love too. You lived giving your all and loving through every toxic encounter because "giving up" wasn't in the cards you dealt, because you knew firsthand how it felt to lose.

I don't think we talk enough about the trauma of not feeling good enough. Never feel like what we give is enough because we constantly need to always give more to get an effort. Never feeling like we are worthy because we chase every chance at being wanted. We don't often talk about the trauma of accepting someone into your life who isn't meant for you after they've shown you countless times they're the wrong piece, but you try and mold yourself into what they need. That ounce of love they gave was enough to cave. We don't often talk about that. We don't talk about the unhealthy yearning of being loved that we'd do anything to feel it. We would let anyone who feels comfort. We don't talk about how it starts with security and ends up with uncertainty. We don't talk about the toxic hold we put on others when we use them to feel something when they're incapable of delivering and we feel damaged. We don't talk about the fear of letting go because we inhale the festering aroma of our gaslighting performer... we fear never feeling the mirage they handled with care again. We don't talk about the burnouts and bareness of picking up the pieces, the fear of actually feeling something real. We don't talk about how the hopeless romantic can lose hope.

We forget to talk about the parts we adapt
in the cycles of our hearts abuse and how
we form these patterns by not wanting to.
My wanting to feel love, that's on me but
when they take advantage of my fragile
heart... that's when the tables turn.
Accepting someone in my life when the
signs have proven they're not for me, that's
on me, but when they use my love for them
as a pawn that's where I draw the line. We
often blame someone else for all the pain we
endure we forget to take accountability for
our part in our heartache. It's true, we set
these expectations for everyone because we
want to feel the experience of a soul
connection. We're left damaged, sensitive,
and guarded when someone tries to walk in
after. We don't talk about how we sacrificed
it all for love when it was never love, it's the
illusion of what we manipulated ourselves
*to believe love to be and how dangerous it
became to be.*

The trauma you're holding from years will always impact you if you allow it. You can't change what happened but you also can't let it control you. To accept your trauma you need to face it… so it can stop killing you slowly.

You can't be a terrible person because of your trauma. You can't keep hurting others because of your trauma. You can't keep slowly killing yourself with all the bad habits you choose to cope with your trauma. You can't keep blaming yourself for your trauma.

You numbing yourself doesn't make the pain go away. You need to make a choice — let your trauma live your life for you, which can lead to bad decisions. Or you can face it, accept it, and understand it will always be a part of you but know you're not a victim you're a survivor.

I'm an **empath**
I feel too much of everyone.
When I love them
their troubles become mine too.
I try to heal them from their trauma.
It's my love language
that's why it's important for me
to release you
If you're not bettering yourself.
It's not love
If I lose myself loving you.

Steps to Healing:

Be honest with yourself.
Be open-minded when it comes to seeing
from all perspectives.
Admit to your trauma.
Learn your triggers.
Unlearn patterns,
Set boundaries.

Healing isn't forgetting your trauma, it's
confronting it and being able to understand
it happened and it can't hug you tight any
longer. Forgiveness is different for
everyone — you decide what you think best
suits your healing journey.

What are your steps to healing?

- _____

- _____

- _____

- _____

- _____

- _____

- _____

- _____

- _____

What is healing for you?

_____

_____

_____

_____

_____

_____

_____

_____

_____

_____

_____

_____

_____

_____

_____

After being in a bad relationship you shouldn't jump right into another until you heal those broken parts of you so you don't repeat past pain. There's no final healing moment, but once you confront your trauma the weight will feel lighter. You don't heal to forget. You heal so you don't repeat or allow past patterns to become a new cycle. It's important to do the work and to go into relationships being aware of your trauma, if you don't, you will potentially hurt yourself or someone else. I speak from a place of experience... nothing I say is easy, this has been years of healing for me.

What is your trauma(s)?

_____

_____

_____

_____

_____

_____

_____

_____

_____

_____

_____

_____

_____

_____

_____

_____

_____

Are you suppressing your trauma?

How long? Why?

_____

_____

_____

_____

_____

_____

_____

_____

_____

_____

_____

_____

_____

_____

_____

_____

_____

We've all been through something heartbreakingly tragic... it's not fair to act like your pain weighs heavier than someone else's just because they've found a place between comfort and healing. Before you judge someone's trauma and healing, don't forget the journey it took to find peace.

Heartbreak Paradox

I was codependent with trauma,
I created this bond with heartbreak.
I thrived in chaos,
I didn't feel purpose without it.
My ideal love
Was to heal the broken,
Without it I was nothing.
Once I healed them
I served my purpose.
The errors of love I wrote into my life
To search for it within the broken
Once I healed them,
I was left with nothing.

To my younger self,

You deserved so much more. You were showered with so much love but you focused on the love you didn't get — you didn't deserve to feel the emptiness that came with certain people in your past. You deserved to be understood and heard, instead, you hid in the shadows because you isolated yourself when misunderstood. Your shyness was a joke to many who didn't try to understand or give you a chance to be yourself. You were quiet, reserved, and down to earth. You couldn't grasp who you were because everyone always told you. You were naïve. You were misguided. You were looking for love in all the wrong safe spaces and the wrong hearts. You created walls that were easily broken down because you wanted to be needed. You let the same people hurt you and come back because your heart was too big and easily forgiving. You wanted to give the same chances you'd want in return, except you never hurt anyone as you've been through. You became riddled with anxiety, you hid from the world — being mute and only open to those you felt a connection to. It was a blessing in disguise, your story is what made you.

Write a letter to your younger self:

_____

_____

_____

_____

_____

_____

_____

_____

_____

_____

_____

_____

_____

_____

_____

_____

_____

_____

Letters from my Inner-child

You are a force out of this world. You deserve everything you've worked hard for. Your passion can only be duplicated by those who feel the same frequency — it's rare, like your heart's language. I don't hold regret for the past time when you were lost… your growth is the reason. You holding yourself accountable for your deception helped too. Having those honest self-talks. Being uncomfortable and facing everything you were suppressing… you are brave and that kind of courage goes a long way. Having faith and accepting forgiveness. Setting boundaries and unlearning patterns. You decided one day you deserved better, so you stopped settling and chose yourself. I always told you that self-love would always be the love to save you… now look at you.

Write a letter to your current self:

_____

_____

_____

_____

_____

_____

_____

_____

_____

_____

_____

_____

_____

_____

_____

_____

_____

_____

I created my safe place in souls who were trauma-bonded like me, to feel familiar, maybe even help them heal so I could forget about my suffering. Being the savior made me feel superior, it made me feel needed... something I never felt. My trauma sunk me deeper into this cycle of self-destruction when I couldn't save anyone and they ended up being a threat to my heart. Trauma bonded us but it left us empty and not empowered. It left us even more broken.

I felt safe surrounded by those who were struggling to fight their demons because I could find myself in them, alone and afraid... but somehow I felt smaller.

My safe place now is surrounded by love, bliss, and reciprocity in the form of peace. I only keep souls around me who aren't damaged by my healing. I've unlearned the patterns of being a savior and learned the biggest lesson, no one could be healed unless they put in the world themselves. I had to stop finding myself in others because it was an excuse to feel smaller, to hide from my own trauma. I surround myself with people who adore me more, who listen and inspire me to be my own, and who appreciate who I am at the core of my being. I surround myself in spaces that don't compete, compare, or diminish my ability to love. I don't surround myself with anyone who makes me feel hard to love.

*Describe your "safe space" in the **past** and how you created it:*

_____

_____

_____

_____

_____

_____

_____

_____

_____

_____

_____

_____

_____

_____

_____

_____

Describe your "safe place" **now** *and how you created it:*

_____

_____

_____

_____

_____

_____

_____

_____

_____

_____

_____

_____

_____

_____

_____

One thing I wished loved ones understood...

Take me as I am, don't assume or try to write me as the version you want me to be. Love me for who I am, not the potential friend or lover you wanted me to be. I've connected with many through forces that couldn't be denied but I felt we lost time because I wasn't recognized or felt on the level I was given. I learned to dim myself and become the version they wanted me to be because I never wanted to lose their love. I became codependent on their codependency without realizing it. I wish the ones who loved me would have loved me — the inner and every layer of me, so I didn't need to lose myself trying to be accepted by everyone who I loved.

Write about one thing
you wished your loved ones understood
about you:

_____

_____

_____

_____

_____

_____

_____

_____

_____

_____

_____

_____

_____

_____

_____

_____

_____

May you continue to grow and heal
And unlearn those toxic traits,
And leave your trauma in the past.

You have a choice,
to continue letting it control you
and every experience
Until you understand it
Until you take control

- *It doesn't define you*

I believe someone who doesn't love themselves completely can love someone else, but it won't be healthy. After so much trauma, how do you love someone, and receive love, without truly understanding what it feels like to be loved — when you can't even stand to love yourself?

When someone blocks their trauma, loving you will be hard. Their trauma will revisit in different ways. Everything that goes wrong will be your fault because of the manipulation to make you believe it's you. They love you but never at full capacity if they never conquer those demons.

How many connections broke because you or someone you loved couldn't face their trauma?

_____

_____

_____

_____

_____

_____

_____

_____

_____

_____

_____

_____

_____

_____

_____

_____

Take accountability for the things you say
when you're mad instead of brushing them
off. Blaming your trauma isn't an apology.
No one deserves to feel worthless only
because you chose to destruct letting your
trauma conquer you instead of
communicating it through.

Take accountability for the things you've said when you were mad:

_____

_____

_____

_____

_____

_____

_____

_____

_____

_____

_____

_____

_____

_____

_____

_____

_____

Taking accountability for all the things I've said when I was hurt and reflected with anger. I said uncomfortable things I meant at the moment but didn't think through. I don't regret any feeling I've ever felt. I only wish I could have taken the time and sat with my thoughts before I reacted. A lot of lost connections because of my lack of empathy, and my selfishness. A lot of connections are broken due to matched energy. I never wanted karma in the worst way, now I think before I speak... I won't allow my temporary emotions to create a monster out of me.

Forgiveness to me isn't about
forgiving someone for the sake of moving
forward with my life. I don't believe
everyone deserves forgiveness, especially
those who have tortured me with the loss of
never forgetting the scar they left me with. I
don't believe in forgiving people who aren't
sorry, especially when sorry is a word often
used without action to hold it. At one point
in my life, I forgave everyone for the sake of
myself in hopes it would make the weight
of my trauma lighter and the memory
would fade with their apology until I
realized every time I looked at them I
couldn't unfeel or forget the depression that
stuck around longer than I wish because I
couldn't figure out how to cope. I believe
forgiveness was healing until I didn't heal.
Forgiving someone who will never
understand the pain you feel is pointless
when they put you through it without any
care. Forgiving someone who murdered my

thought of love and caused me to lose myself didn't help me recover. It wasn't until I took my power back that and realized their forgiveness was to ease their guilt. Forgiving myself for allowing them to destroy me. Forgiving myself for allowing myself to create a bond over the trauma. Forgiving myself for allowing myself to believe everyone who said they loved me had the best intentions—some only were out to break me.

What does forgiveness mean to you?

_____

_____

_____

_____

_____

_____

_____

_____

_____

_____

_____

_____

_____

_____

_____

_____

_____

_____

_____

Past experiences need to be worked out within you because opening yourself to someone new. Make your new partner aware of your past so no old patterns are repeated. Don't expect them to come into your life and heal you of all the trauma and heartache — no one can heal you but you.

When you grew up taught one way of something, it's up to you to unlearn patterns, and behaviors, and create new ways. You don't need to be stuck in the past and drowning in your trauma.
It's called growing.

I had to let go of my savior complex to be happy. It wasn't up to me to save anyone from their demons. I wasn't loving them for who they were, I was loving them for who I imagined them to be.

We all have years of trauma we hold onto. A lot of it we blame on the source of when it got planted, but when you start poisoning everyone with it there's no one to blame but you. It's no one's job to heal you but you.

It was years of unpacking trauma. I planted seeds in connections with the same patterns and trust issues… and ended up blaming them when they hurt me when they weren't the ones. I needed to take accountability for holding onto the unhealed before I could be free of it all.

Often we blame our trauma for the many times we end up broken or never fully healed. We have a choice — to forever hold onto that broken piece or to do our best to grow and heal… to make a better life than what we were afraid of.
It's a long journey. A journey that needs constant work and awareness. To live knowing it was something that destroyed you but you were able to set yourself free and build a version of yourself that you always knew you could be… without the fear holding you back.

It's the beginning of another journey
Healing is messy,
It's not immediate peace

It's time to unlearn everything
You've made a pattern,
while holding on to the trauma
for as long as you can remember.

Choose to bloom.

I want to thank you for reading this collection. I'm always honored when someone takes the time to check out my work... even more, when they decide to purchase my work and listen to the voice I silenced for so long... the one I'm slowly freeing through the years. Writing has saved my life and helped me heal all these years. Writing down every feeling helped me understand my emotions and the motions they go through. My trauma doesn't define me — what I once feared is what I'm healing from... where I'm at in my journey is always better than where I once was. It's always a work in progress because I believe there's always something new to find within myself...

All platforms:

Instagram: Moonsoulchild
Facebook: Moonsoulchild
Tiktok: Bymoonsoulchild
Twitter: Bymoonsoulchild
Apple Music: Moonsoulchild
Spotify: Moonsoulchild

Moonsoulchild.com

The other books in this collection:

Inner-child: Healing from within
Mental Health: Fulfilling You

Anonymous Stories
(submissions by supports)

Here's to sharing our truth

Anonymous 1:

My story about trauma is a personal and private story of myself being traumatized by being forced to abort and murder my unborn child still in my womb at the young age of 17 years old which was painfully forced on me by my biological mother. Against my will. And still to this very day 34 years later, it still haunts and kills me way deep down inside my heart and my mind. I am still struggling with this issue of forgiveness. In forgiving myself and especially forgiving my biological mother.

Anonymous 2:

I grew up unwanted as a child. My family hated me, my father was an alcoholic and my brother turned into one as well. I was the punching bag for the family, the one who took everyone's frustrations. I was called so many names, I felt worthless. I had no confidence and at 32, I still am fighting for confidence. I'm always chasing after another goal to prove myself, even though my parents are deceased and have no contact with my brother, I'm always trying to be good enough. I'm happy to say, I don't drink at all, I have a wonderful career helping others that are in the position I was in.

Anonymous 3:

I am a teenager and I have undiagnosed attachment/ abandonment/ trust issues. These things make my life so hard. I'm afraid to label a person as "a friend" because my inner child has been reminding me that everyone will leave me, abandon me, or they don't care from the start, they're pretending to like me. And as a consequence, I'll be left with a one-sided relationship which is my fear. So I socially isolate myself to defend myself, my inner child. And I'll be distant from you, again and again, every time I can smell the slightest chance of you, leaving first. It's just so tiring for a clingy person like me to have a mindset of "I'll leave you before you've left me", and call it a defense.

Anonymous 4:

They say a person's childhood plays a critical role in their adult life. It's crazy how true that is. I was made from lust, not love. Love is what I yearn for. A deadbeat dad and a mom who put everyone first except for her kids. I lived with my Grandmom. Overbearing, tough-loving one. Not the kind that makes chocolate chip cookies and watched movies with you. The kind that would scream at you for not finishing your food, the kind that would not hesitate to say that you're gaining weight. "Tough love" is a term I grew to hate. I grew up thinking that even if people are mean to you they still love you. Even if people walk out of your life they still love you. That is not love. I've spent my whole 22 years of life searching hoping I can experience some sort of love I have yet to find from a human but I have some expectations of what it might be. I healed from this with self-love. I have a picture of my younger self in my mirror. Sometimes I look in the mirror and want to say cruel things to myself but then I imagine that I'm saying them to little me. The little me who was dealt with a life of things she didn't deserve. It breaks my heart that I want to protect that little girl. It's my job to do it now. Every day is a constant battle, as long as I remain breathing my story remains under construction, I have to make one person happy, and that's the girl in the mirror. Love yourself, so others know how to love you.

Anonymous 5:

Growing up gay, in the closet in a traditional Asian household, I was always told I need to be a man, I am the man of the house, men don't cry, and men need to be strong. I struggled with my identity my whole childhood. I pursued policing, joined the military, and did martial arts (all the "manly" things) to prove to my dad how much of a man I was. My dad was an alcoholic and was so hard on me. In high school, I was vice president of the art club and expressed myself through art but I never saw myself as an artist because I was

so deep in my trauma and conditioned
beliefs of who I needed to be. Now I Am
older and realize that growing up is going
back to doing the things I loved doing
before the world told me who I Am
supposed to be. I left the military to pursue
my art through tattooing and feel like I Am
finally back home to me. Realizing I Am the
Creator of my own life.

Anonymous 6:

From a very young age, my family rejected
me so much and called me all kinds of
things I remember running to the bathroom
and crying because I felt like I was nothing.
My aunts and uncles would tell my cousins
not to be around me as I was bad and
stupid. When I started going to school I was
bullied so much I would cry every time id
have to go to school and again went to the
bathroom and cried.

I had no one to turn to but I had the
bathroom, so quiet and small just like me.

Later on the bathroom and I became good friends, every time I had too much to eat that would make me uglier and more disgusting than I already was I went to purge in my happy place, the bathroom.

Spent countless hours in the bathroom as the shower water would blend in perfectly with tears running down my face I could spend hours googling how to kill myself without it being painful. Oh, the bathroom.

One day, I showered and felt so many things washed away from me and realized all these struggles were just me getting out of my cocoon.

In the same bathroom where I had wept, I suddenly stepped into metamorphosis. The wind that would hold me up under my wings was always there waiting for me, just waiting for me to spread my wings and fly.

I now love myself, I am beautiful and I am whole.

Anonymous 7:

I grew up in a home where there was no
love, affection, or warmth I went out there
and seek for love in the wrong places. I've
never had any luck when it comes to
relationships because it was more of a
sexual situation and getting my heart
broken over and over again because all I
needed was someone reassuring me all the
time that they love me and tell me I'm
pretty for me to believe that I am really
pretty. I've always been so afraid to be alone
because I thought I'd lose myself in the
process of being alone but I actually lost
myself more and more in every relationship
I've been in...And now I look back and I
realize that instead of wasting my time in
all those relationships that broke and
damaged me, I could have used that time to
work on learning how to love myself and
reassuring myself, but than I remind myself
every day that "it's okay. I've made choices
and I've learned and I'm okay." Whatever
decision I took, whatever choices I have
made, have turned me into the strong and
brave person that I am today and I am

happy that I still wake up every day with
the hope that everything is gonna work out
for me and I'll get where I want to and the
only reassurance and love I need right now
is the one coming from me because I know
my heart, I know life, I know my situation
and I know what I've been through and
only I can heal myself

Anonymous 8:

I was sexually abused as a child by a cousin.
I acted out toward my mom, I suppose I
wanted an apology but she never knew it
happened. I still acted out because I felt she
should have known something was wrong.
It happened more than 3 times. Anyway, I
held it all together and eventually got
through school, graduated with honors, and
am currently doing my master's. I am a
teacher. My husband doesn't know about
my ordeal, no one except my family does. I
have 2 sisters who hold me responsible for
my late mom's death due to cancer. Every
time we fight, they bring up how I lashed
out as a child. I'm trying but struggling to
get on with my life due to my strained

relationship with my sisters. They see me as this strong person yet inside I'm dying I'm just not used to showing it, it's been my coping mechanism forever. They failed to understand me it hurts. I was so busy trying to Make it look like I am just normal and never experienced any trauma that they forgot. I'm now at a stage where I feel it's going to break me, close to a nervous breakdown. I apologized to mom for giving her a hard time before she passed I wish they could have helped me when I needed it instead of ignoring it.

10123642R10062